Autumn Life
Coloring Book

An Adult Coloring Book Featuring Beautiful Autumn Scenes, Charming Animals and Relaxing Fall Inspired Landscapes.

an Imprint of **The Fruitful Mind Publishing LTD**.

www.coloringbookcafe.com

Have questions? Let us know.

support@coloringbookcafe.com

 facebook.com/coloringbookcafe

 @coloringbookcafe

This Book
Belongs To:

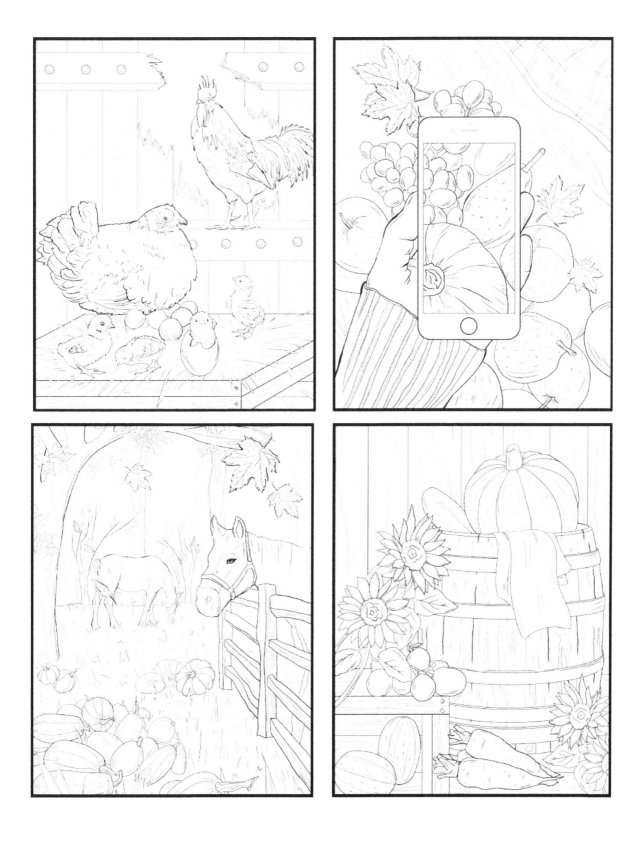

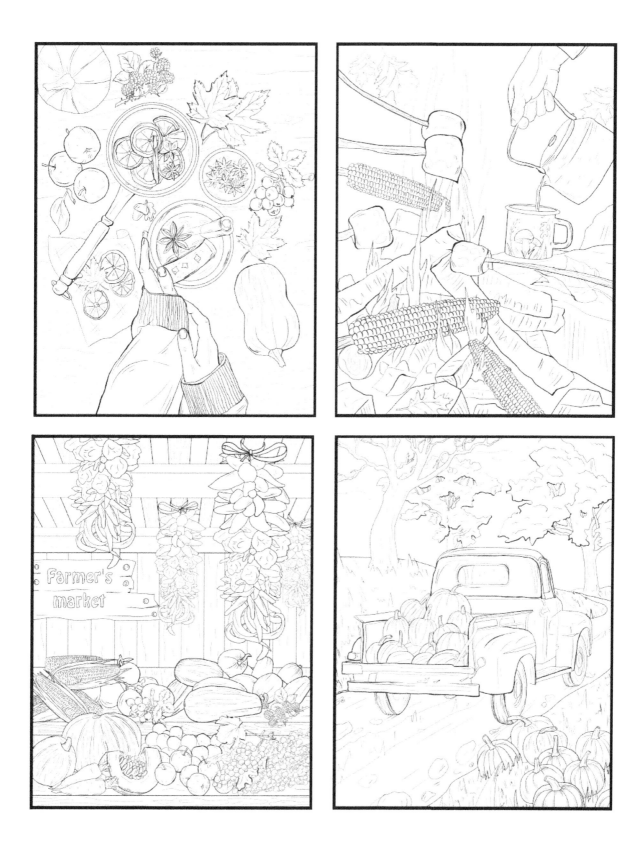

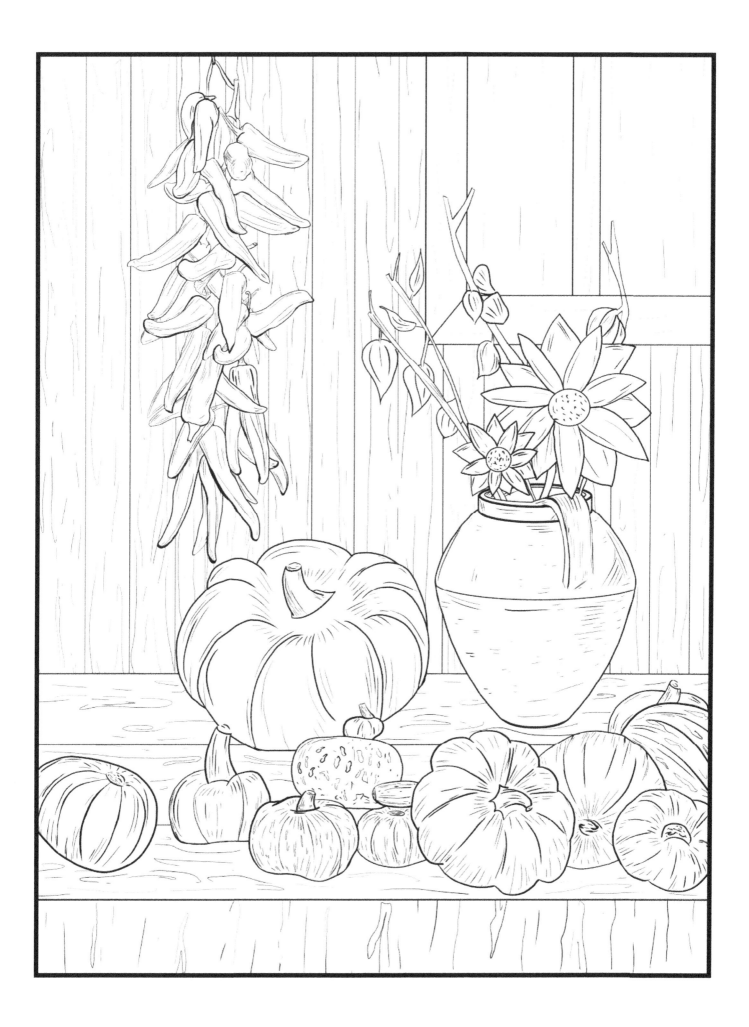

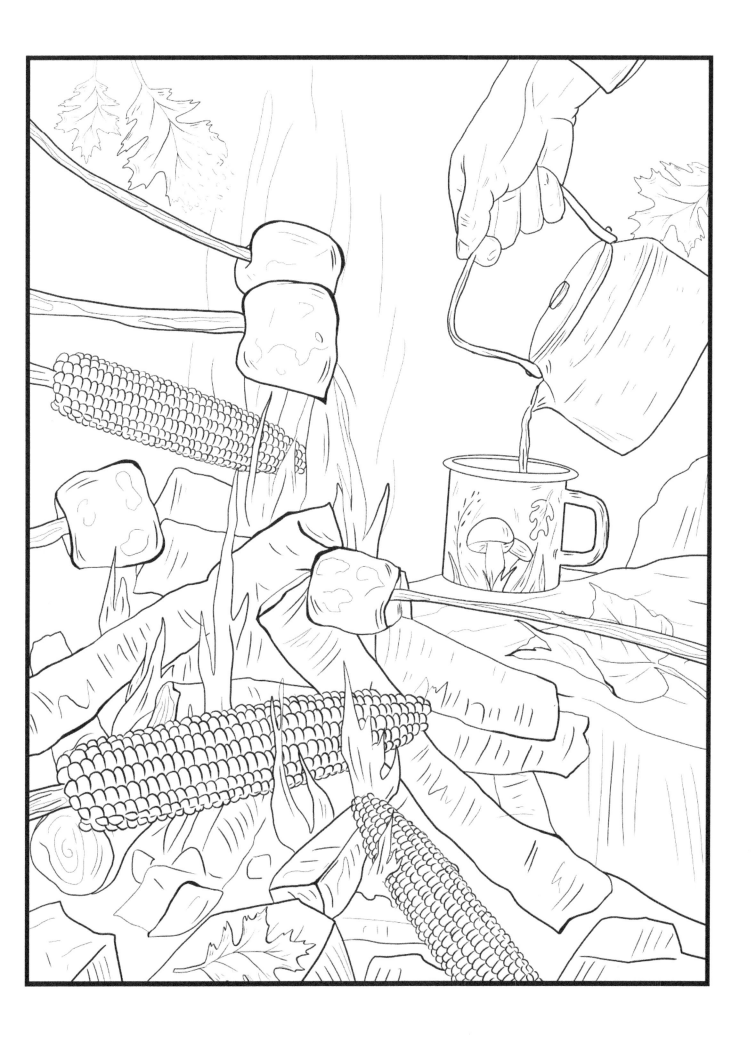

Made in the USA
Coppell, TX
26 October 2020